BABE RUTH

DISCOVER THE LIFE OF AN AMERICAN LEGEND

Don McLeese

Rourke
Publishing LLC
Vero Beach, Florida 32964

www.rourkepublishing.com

PHOTO CREDITS: All photos The Babe Ruth Museum

Cover: *Babe Ruth, New York Yankee, 1925*

Editor: Frank Sloan

Cover design by Nicola Stratford

Library of Congress Cataloging-in-Publication Data

McLeese, Don.

McLeese, Don.
 Babe Ruth / Don McLeese.
     p. cm. — (Discover the life of an American legend)
Summary: A simple biography of one of the best known figures in the history of baseball, home-run hitter Babe Ruth.
Includes bibliographical references (p.) and index.
 ISBN 1-58952-304-0
 1. Ruth, Babe, 1895-1948—Juvenile literature. 2. Baseball players—United States—Biography—Juvenile literature. [1. Ruth, Babe, 1895-1948. 2. Baseball players.] I. Title. II. American legends (Vero Beach, Fla.)
 GV865.R8 M36 2002
 796.357'092--dc21

                                                    2002004095

Printed in the USA

W/W

TABLE OF CONTENTS

The Greatest   5

Babe as a Boy   9

St. Mary's   11

Jack Dunn's "Baby"   13

Boston Babe   14

Yankee Star   16

Babe Loved Kids   19

Hall of Famer   20

Glossary   23

Index   24

Further Reading/Websites to Visit   24

THE GREATEST

Many people think Babe Ruth was the greatest **baseball** player ever. Others say he was the greatest **athlete** in any sport. Before Babe hit 60 **home runs** in 1927, no other player had hit even half that many in a season. Though Mark McGwire and Sammy Sosa have since hit more in a season, Babe led the way.

Babe hits a long one.

Babe Ruth was not only the greatest home run **hitter** baseball had seen. He was also a very good **pitcher**. He might have become the best pitcher in the American League, if he hadn't switched to the **outfield**. Pitchers don't play every game, and his team needed Babe to hit!

He's safe at the plate!

BABE AS A BOY

George Herman Ruth, Jr., was born in Baltimore on February 6, 1895. His parents, George and Kate, ran a bar. He grew up in the bar, and his parents worked long hours. He became a wild boy. His parents didn't know how to make him behave.

An early photo of
George Herman Ruth

ST. MARY'S

When George Jr. was seven, his parents sent him to St. Mary's Industrial School for Boys. Many of the boys there were **orphans** who had no parents. The school made Babe behave and taught him how to play baseball. He could hit and throw the ball farther than any of the older boys.

JACK DUNN'S "BABY"

Young George left St. Mary's when he was 18. By then he was known as Baltimore's best young athlete. Jack Dunn owned the Baltimore Orioles, and he signed George Jr. to play for the team. Sportswriters called him "Jack Dunn's Baby," which was shortened to "Babe." Everyone called him "Babe" Ruth.

Babe with the Orioles
(front row, 3rd from left)   13

BOSTON BABE

Babe became a member of the American League's Boston Red Sox in 1914. He was one of the team's top pitchers, helping the Red Sox finish first in 1915, 1916, and 1918. But he was also a great hitter. In 1919, he hit 29 home runs. The rest of the team hit only four!

Babe pitched for the Red Sox.

YANKEE STAR

Babe joined the New York Yankees in 1920, and he became an even bigger star. With Babe, the team almost always finished first in the American League and often won the World Series.

The Yankees built a new baseball field in 1923. It was called Yankee Stadium. Babe Ruth was so popular, however, that it was often called "The House That Ruth Built."

Babe became baseball's greatest hitter.

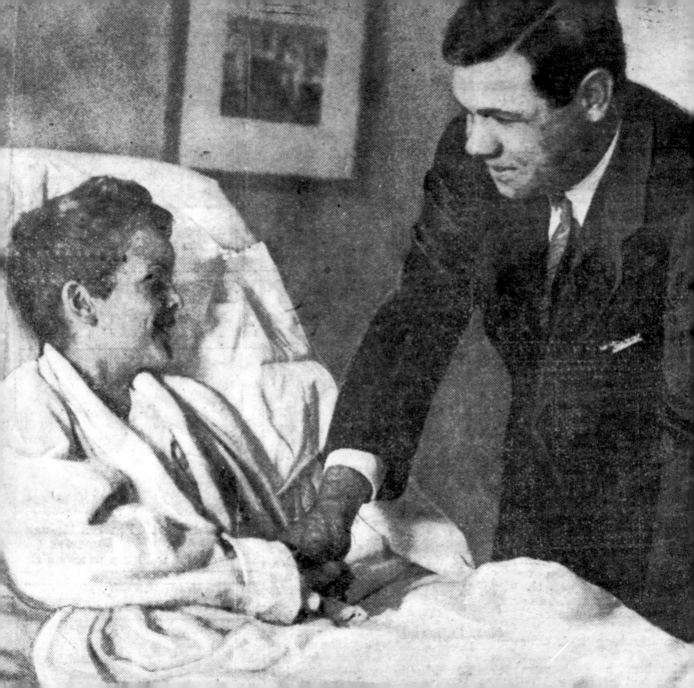

BABE LOVED KIDS

Because his own childhood was so hard, Babe was kind to children. He once visited an 11-year-old boy in the hospital. The boy was very sick. Babe promised the boy, Johnny Sylvester, that he'd hit a home run just for him. The next game, he hit two home runs! Johnny got better.

HALL OF FAMER

When Babe retired from baseball in 1935, he held every record as baseball's best home run hitter. Four years later, the National Baseball **Hall of Fame** elected Babe as one of its first members.

Babe (front row, 2nd from left) at the Hall of Fame's opening

Babe Ruth died of cancer on August 16, 1948. On any list of famous athletes, Babe Ruth ranks near the top.

GLOSSARY

athlete (ATH leet) — a person who plays sports.

baseball (BAYSE bal) — a sport played with a ball and bat.

Hall of Fame (HALL uv FAYM) — place where the best players in a sport (or the best at anything) are honored.

hitter (HIT ur) — the batter; the baseball player who hits the ball with his bat

home runs (HOHM RUNZ) — hits in baseball that let the batter go all the way around the bases and score a run.

orphans (OR funz) — people whose parents are both dead.

outfield (OUT feeld) — in baseball, right, left, and center fields.

pitcher (PIT chur) — the baseball player who throws the ball to the hitter.

INDEX

"Babe" (nickname) 13
Baltimore Orioles 13
Boston Red Sox 14
Dunn, Jack 13
McGwire, Mark 5
New York Yankees 16
National Baseball
    Hall of Fame 20
parents 9
St. Mary's Industrial School
    for Boys 11, 13
Sosa, Sammy 5
Sylvester, Johnny 19
Yankee Stadium 16

Further Reading

Brandt, Keith. *Babe Ruth: Home Run Hero*. Troll Communication, L.L.C., 1997.
Burleigh, Robert. *Home Run: The Story of Babe Ruth*. Silver Whistle/Harcourt Brace, 1998.
Jacobs, William Jay. *They Shaped the Game*. Simon & Schuster, 1994.

Websites To Visit

http://www.baberuthmuseum.com/html/client_frames.asp
http://www.baberuth.com/

About The Author

Don McLeese is an award-winning journalist whose work has appeared in many newspapers and magazines. He is a frequent contributor to the World Book Encyclopedia. He and his wife, Maria, have two daughters and live in West Des Moines, Iowa.